T0019918

THE LITTLE
BOOK FOR
MODERN
WITCHES

ASTRID
CARVEL

summersdale

A LITTLE BOOK FOR MODERN WITCHES

Text by Stephanie Drane

An Hachette UK Company
www.hachette.co.uk

Summersdale Publishers Ltd
Part of Octopus Publishing Group Limited
Carmelite House
50 Victoria Embankment
LONDON
EC4Y 0DZ
UK

www.summersdale.com

Printed and bound in China

ISBN: 978-1-80007-929-8

Substantial discounts on bulk quantities of Summersdale books are available to corporations, professional associations and other organizations. For details contact general enquiries: telephone: +44 (0) 1243 771107 or email: enquiries@summersdale.com.

Disclaimer
The author and the publisher cannot accept responsibility for any misuse or misunderstanding of any information contained herein, or any loss, damage or injury, be it health or otherwise, suffered by any individual or group acting upon or relying on information contained herein.

CONTENTS

INTRODUCTION

Claiming the word "witch" to describe yourself is a powerful thing to do. It's an acknowledgement of your inner power and a recognition of your ability to master the direction of your intention and energy to manifest your desires. You don't need any special initiation ceremony or training to be a witch (although both can be enriching and beautiful experiences); you just need to know in your heart that you are one.

This book welcomes you to dive into your witchcraft practice, or create one, offering crafts, spells and suggestions to make your magic effective. It will encourage you to use your own intuition, ideas and energy to customize and empower your spell craft because the most essential power a witch has is their personal energy. The most important knowledge, meanwhile, is your self-understanding and your intentions.

It is widely believed that the intentions you put out are sent back threefold, so if you send out goodwill, it will return to you tripled, and the same goes for negative intentions. Witches, therefore, grow wise in all the implications of exerting their will.

Luckily, as a witch, you also have the magical forces of nature at your fingertips! Within these pages, you will find some ideas on using natural ingredients that can lend wisdom and magic to your spells. A vital component of witchcraft is understanding the natural energies that flow through all nature, which are not owned or controlled by anyone, meaning witchcraft is for everyone, regardless of age, gender, sexuality, ethnicity or ability. All you need is a willing heart, an open mind, and to believe that you are capable of magic!

AN INTRODUCTION TO WHITE WITCHCRAFT

Does the word "witch" stir something within you, calling you to its mystery and magic? Read on to delve into the world of white witchcraft, its history and its benefits. Discover the natural energies that empower your craft and the importance of your inner power in walking your own witchy path.

WHAT IS WITCHCRAFT?

Witchcraft is the practice of using your personal will and intention along with the natural energies around you for magical purposes.

Witches usually feel a deep connection to, and love of, nature. Modern witchcraft has its roots in ancient Paganism, from a time when nature was seen as sacred and a manifestation of the Divine spirit, with each part of nature – tree, rock, creature, plant, etc. – having its own magical properties and vital role to play. A witch can harness the natural wisdom and magical properties of nature and use them in spells and rituals to manifest desires, heal and create positive change.

A witch's magic is powered by their personal energy, spirit and intentions. The magical purposes of witchcraft are many and varied but include healing and attracting blessings such as love and wealth or for protection and luck.

WHITE WITCHCRAFT

White witchcraft is a term used to describe using magic only for good. These days it is more common for witches to practise magic for themselves and only for others with their permission because what one person sees as kindness may be seen as unhelpful or inappropriate by another.

The Wiccan Rede "An' it harm none do what ye will" (meaning do whatever you like as long as no one is harmed) serves as a good reminder for your practice. So think through the consequences of your actions from all angles and be mindful of how you might unintentionally cause harm by only thinking of yourself or the individual you are casting a spell for.

Modern white witchcraft has become a popular form of self-help as it is about focusing on inner power, being mindful of nature and empowering yourself to create a nourishing spiritual practice – all things that are a balm to the pressures of a hectic modern lifestyle.

THE HISTORY OF WITCHCRAFT

The history of witchcraft has tendrils running back to more recent Wiccan practices and further through folk magic, deep into the beliefs of pre-Christian times when many people worshipped nature and the spirits they believed dwelt within all things. What we now think of as "magic" has been part of everyday life in one way or another at various times throughout history and it was used to explain and control natural phenomena, heal the sick, commune with ancestors, divine the future and for a myriad of other purposes.

With the advent of organized religion, the Pagan practices of worshipping nature and many deities began to be associated with evil and devil worship. People became mistrustful of those who lived on the edges of society or used folk magic and their knowledge of natural remedies to heal and help others. Often, midwives and healers, elders or "seers" who might previously have been respected community figures became scapegoats. Misfortune was wrongly blamed on witchcraft, and many thousands were put to death during the witch trials in Europe and America in the sixteenth and seventeenth centuries.

New laws in the UK in 1951, meaning it was no longer illegal to practise witchcraft, led to many new forms of witchcraft. This included Gardnerian Wicca, established by Gerald Gardner, an amateur scholar of magic who claimed initiation into a coven in the New Forest in the 1930s, and Alexandrian Wicca, developed in the 1960s by Alex and Maxine Sanders, who trained under Gardner. The worship of goddesses and gods and respectful care for nature inherent in modern witchcraft made sense to many who were craving a more equal and environmentally aware society. Witchcraft has spread and evolved, and today there are almost as many forms of witchcraft as there are witches.

One of the attractions of witchcraft is that individuals can create their own spiritual path and while there are covens and neopagan religions, individuality is primarily respected and celebrated.

WITCH WITH RESPECT

Modern witchcraft is often an eclectic practice, meaning many aspects – such as spells, divination, rituals, offerings, words of power and protective charms – have their roots in various cultures and traditions. It is important to remember that the words "witch" and "witchcraft" have been (and still are in some instances) used to vilify, marginalize and persecute many indigenous peoples as well as people who are different or threatening to the status quo. It is essential not to take for granted the freedom that you have to practise witchcraft and be mindful of respecting the origins and cultures from which you borrow to build your practice. The path of a witch is winding and mystical, so be open to trying new magic and respect those whose craft is different to yours.

WITCH YOUR WAY

The beautiful thing about witchcraft is that it draws on your inherent powers and wisdom, and you can create your own personal practice and use it to enhance your life. As an individual practice, witchcraft can look different from witch to witch. Don't compare yourself to others unfavourably or assume that other witches' practices will look like yours.

When you see the positive effects of using your inner power to exert your will and manifest your desires, your confidence and self-esteem will grow, empowering you to create the life you want and helping you become your best self.

Acting on intuition is another way to build your confidence and self-understanding, boosting your inner power. This personal power fuels your magic, so always follow your intuition and the whispers of your heart.

*The first time I called myself
a "witch" was the most
magical moment of my life.*

MARGOT ADLER

YOUR
THOUGHTS
AND WORDS
HAVE MAGIC
POWER

WITCH'S TOOLKIT

It is important to note that you don't actually need anything other than your own intention and inner power to be a witch and to cast a spell. However, by their very nature, many witches are drawn to exciting, mystical objects like crystals and wands, herbs and natural objects. And they do have magical uses as well as making you feel "witchy"!

Making "mundane" objects magical by the will of your heart adds that little bit more of your personal power to any spell. For example, a gorgeous pink-hued pebble you spotted and lovingly collected from the beach can have just as much energy as a rose quartz crystal.

To "consecrate" any object for use in spells, hold it in your hands and visualize your energy entering it. Tell the object how it is significant to you and how its magic will help you. You can also charge objects with energy this way. Another way to charge tools and crystals is to leave them in the moonlight or sunlight to absorb lunar or solar energy.

Spell ingredients, tools and the time you cast a spell are chosen for their magical or symbolic properties, which are called "correspondences". You can find many lists of correspondences in books and online, but a few basics are included on pages 20–21

TOOLS

Wand

A wand is often a wooden stick used to direct energy and intention. Use a wand to cast a protective magic circle to carry out your spells and rituals by "drawing" a circle around you in the air. Different types of wood lend their own natural wisdom and magical properties to the wand, as do any crystals or other natural objects used to adorn the wand. You can make and decorate your own wand (see page 28) or simply pick up a stick that you are drawn to and use that.

Cauldron

Cauldrons are used for creating potions, burning herbs and incense, gathering, storing and charging spell ingredients, and burning spells. Traditional cauldrons come in various sizes, but despite giving you intense witchy vibes, an actual cauldron is not necessary. A cooking pot is a good substitute, or use a heatproof dish, bucket, bowl or basket, depending on your purposes.

Besom

A witch riding on her besom (broom) is a familiar image, but the besom is intended for magical protection and purification. Use a besom to sweep out negative energy from your home or before casting a magic circle. Sweep a small besom over your altar to cleanse the energy there or around your body to brush off negative energy (see page 26).

Altar

An altar is a sacred space for performing spells and divination, celebrating the seasons and honouring deities. Your altar can be any size or shape, be permanent or temporary and be as simple or elaborate as you wish. Start with a few symbolic objects such as candles, crystals and natural objects (shells, feathers, etc.) and build from there.

Grimoire

A grimoire or book of shadows is a journal for recording magical information you have picked up, such as lore, spells, charms and potions.

MAGICAL CORRESPONDENCES

Correspondences are the associations between spell ingredients and their magical qualities. Choose the ingredients and timing of your spell so that you can draw on their natural wisdom and innate magic.

Colours

Use colours that suit your spell:

- Red – passion, love, ambition, anger, vibrancy
- Orange – success, confidence, strength, justice
- Yellow – intellect, memory, charm, imagination
- Green – fertility, harmony, healing, prosperity
- Pink – romance, peace, positivity, nurturing
- Blue – communication, calmness, trust, soothing
- Purple – spirituality, power, wisdom, foresight

Time

Choose the best time to cast your spell:

- New moon – beginning new things
- Waxing moon – growth, attraction, inspiration
- Full moon – femininity, love, knowledge, prosperity, divination
- Waning moon – removal, banishing, releasing and letting go
- Monday – money
- Tuesday – courage

- Wednesday – communication
- Thursday – luck
- Friday – love
- Saturday – discipline
- Sunday – joy

Herbs and spices

Using these kitchen favourites to evoke their qualities turns cooking into spellcasting.

- Basil – prosperity and inner strength
- Parsley – fertility and honesty
- Bay – wisdom, foresight, strength and good fortune
- Cinnamon – love, comfort, power and success
- Black pepper – purification, inner strength and protection
- Sage – cleansing and protection
- Oregano – health and happiness
- Cardamom – love and friendship
- Chilli – passion, virility and inspiration
- Rosemary – purification, positivity and memory
- Thyme – concentration and business success
- Allspice – compassion, luck and healing

The correspondences noted here are just a small example of the properties of each ingredient. Some herbs and spices have many uses, which vary according to tradition and culture.

CRAFTS AND MAKES

Buying witchy tools and decorations is fun, but creating your own imbues them with your energy and intention, making them more powerful. Tweak any of the crafts in this chapter to suit your needs and switch any equipment listed for whatever you have to hand. Get witch-crafting and enjoy!

HAG STONE PENDANT

Sometimes called holy stones or adder stones, hag stones have a hole through them and are often considered protective. To wear and carry this protection with you, you will need to find yourself a suitable stone, so when you're at the beach, remember to keep your eyes open and ask Mother Nature to help you find the right stone for you.

You will need

- Small hag stone
- Suitable chain, ribbon, string, leather thong or even a shoelace

Method

1. Pick a smooth stone with a hole in it of a suitable size to hang around your neck.

2. Thread the stone onto your necklace (chain, ribbon, string, leather, lace, etc.).

3. As you fasten the ends of your chosen necklace together, hold in your mind the intention that this act is forming a protective circle that will keep you safe while you are wearing it.

> You can charge your pendant in sunlight as a charm against the winter blues. Wear throughout the dark season to connect you to the sun's energy and remind you that light days will return (see page 108).

MINI BESOM

A besom is a witch's broom, used to clean and sweep away negative energy. Make your own small besom to cleanse your space. You can keep this on your altar and use it by sweeping it to get rid of unwanted energy.

You will need

- Stick to use as the besom handle (choose a length that suits your purpose)
- Secateurs
- Bunch of smaller twigs for the bristles
- String, wire or ribbon

Optional extras

- Dried lavender or other herbs
- Small charm or natural object such as a shell or acorn for decoration (again, choose to suit your needs)
- Glue or string

Method

1. Cut your handle stick to the required length.

2. Trim your bunch of smaller twigs to roughly half the length of the handle.

3. If using dried herbs, cut these to the length of the bunch of twigs and add them to the bundle.

4. Insert the end of the handle into the centre of the bunch of twigs and secure it by tying it tightly with string, wire or ribbon and fix it in place with a bit of glue if needed.

5. If using a decorative charm or natural object, glue or tie this to your besom.

WAND

A handcrafted wand is potent. You might choose a type of wood that grows in your favourite place, blossoms in your birth month or for its correspondences. Find a windblown stick or ask permission from a tree in your garden to cut a stick and leave an offering of thanks in return.

You will need

- Wooden stick
- Saw or knife

Optional extras

- Sandpaper
- Leather thong, ribbon, wool or anything suitable for binding
- Crystals, shells, feathers, pebbles
- Charms in "witchy" shapes, such as pentacles, stars or moons
- Paint or marker pens
- Glue

Method

1. Taking care, use the saw or knife to cut your stick to the length you desire (traditionally from the tips of your fingers to your elbow), cutting away from your body.

2. If you wish to whittle off any knobbly bits or bark, use the knife and sandpaper and carefully do so.

3. If you want a comfortable handle, bind one end with leather, wool or ribbon. Tie or glue in place.

4. Add any further decorations that you like.

5. Consecrate and charge your wand (see pages 16–17).

SPELL JARS

Witches seem drawn to small bottles and jars, so you might already have a collection. Thrift pretty jars or reuse attractive food and drink containers. Fill them with herbs, crystals and other magic ingredients to create spells for many uses.

You will need

- Small glass jar or bottle with a lid or stopper
- Quartz crystal to suit your spell (e.g. rose quartz for love)
- Range of ingredients such as salt, sugar, herbs and spices, chosen for their magic powers (e.g. allspice for compassion)
- Natural objects (shells, acorns, seeds, etc.)
- Slip of paper
- Pen
- Candle (colour-suited to your spell, if you like)

Method

1. Choose items to put in your spell bottle based on the natural wisdom they will bring to your spell. Place them mindfully inside the bottle.

2. If you wish, write your intention for the spell onto the slip of paper. Roll it into a scroll and pop it in the bottle.

3. Seal the lid or stopper with candle wax if you wish. Choose the colour candle to suit your requirements or use white as a good all-rounder. Light the candle and drip the wax over the lid to seal it.

4. Carry the spell jar with you, or keep it in a place in your home that is relevant to the spell.

5. Once the spell has worked, you can either keep the jar or dispose of the contents by burying or burning them safely.

THE EARTH IS AT
YOUR FEET;

THE UNIVERSE
IS AT YOUR
FINGERTIPS;

MAGIC IS IN
YOUR SOUL

*The world is full of magic
things patiently waiting for
our senses to grow sharper.*

W. B. YEATS

RUNES

Runes are Norse symbols possibly dating back as far as 200 BCE. Each symbol has a specific meaning, and runes can be "read" for divination and insights.

You will need

- Air-dry clay
- Toothpick or similar tool for drawing in clay
- Paint or marker pen (optional)

Method

1. Take an acorn-sized piece of clay and roll it into a ball.

2. Press the clay flat with your hand to create a disc shape.

3. Draw a rune symbol on it with the toothpick. Repeat steps 1–3 until you have all 24 runes.

4. It is not traditional, but you can add a blank clay disc representing destiny or fate if you wish.

5. Pick out the inscribed symbols with a fine paintbrush or marker pen if you like.

Rune meanings

Fehu
prosperity

Uruz
health

Thurisaz
opposition

Ansuz
inspiration

Raidho
travel/journey

Kenaz
creativity

Gebo
gifts

Wunjo
relationships

Hagalaz
transformation

Nauthiz
resistance

Isa
constraint

Jera
rewards

Eihwaz
unknown influences

Pertho
joy

Algiz
oversight

Sowilo
guidance

Tiwaz
intellect

Berkano
growth

Ehwaz
work

Mannuz
state of mind

Laguz
balance

Ingwaz
contemplation

Othala
family

Dagaz
synchronicity

PENTAGRAM FOR PROTECTION

Generally considered the emblem of witchcraft, a pentagram is a five-pointed star traditionally drawn in a single uninterrupted line starting at the top down to the bottom left point. The points represent the elements of earth, air, fire, water and spirit. The pentagram has protective qualities, and many witches wear them or hang them in their homes for that reason.

You will need

- 5 sticks of equal length (choose the length according to the size of the pentagram you wish to make)
- String
- Glue (optional)

Method

1. Lay your sticks out in a pentagram shape.
2. Secure each point by tying the sticks together. Use glue to strengthen the joints if necessary.
3. Add a hanging loop of string to the top point.

Practise drawing a pentagram in one go without lifting the pen from the page. Use your wand or finger to draw a pentagram in the air around you or onto your car, clothes or purse for protection.

SPELL
PROFILES

The most essential ingredients in any spell are your intention and the personal energy you put into it. There are spells for all sorts of purposes in this chapter; draw on your intuition to add to or change them to suit your exact desires.

CASTING A MAGIC CIRCLE

The magic circle is a sacred space created by witches to perform their spells and rituals. Within the circle, you are separated from the mundane world and protected from negative energy outside. You don't have to cast a circle for every spell; just when it feels right.

1. Face north and point the finger of your dominant hand or hold and point a wand.

2. Walk deosil (clockwise), drawing an imaginary circle around you. If outdoors, scratch it into the earth. You can also mark the circle boundary with salt, chalk, flower petals or herbs.

3. Visualize a sphere of energy forming around you as you cast your circle.

4. If you wish, mark the compass directions and "call in the quarters". To do so, place a stone just inside the circle boundary in the direction of north and say, "Spirit of the north, element of earth, you are honoured in this circle." Repeat this for the other three elements by placing a feather in the east for air, a candle in the south for fire and a shell in the west for water. Change the words to honour each direction and element.

A SIMPLE NOURISHING SPELL

Add an extra sprinkle of magic to your home cooking with this spell.

Light a candle while cooking your meal. A white candle is good, or you could look up colour correspondences and choose a coloured candle to match your particular situation or needs, for example, green for abundance or pink for love. Place your candle somewhere safe, and never leave it unattended. The light from the candle represents the love and positivity you wish to enter your food.

Casting the spell

1. While you cook, hold the intention that the meal will be full of goodness and nourishment for your body, mind and soul.

2. If you need to stir your recipe, stir deosil (clockwise) and visualize light pouring from your hand, through the spoon and into your food.

3. You can also look up the correspondences of herbs and spices and add them, as appropriate, to invoke those qualities. A few common ingredients and some of their magical properties are listed on page 21.

CANDLE MAGIC

Try this easy divination spell by lighting a candle and holding your purpose in mind as you light it.

You can elaborate on this spell by incorporating other steps – here are some you might like to try:

- Choose a coloured candle that corresponds to your intention (see page 20).

- Dedicate the candle to your purpose by inscribing words or symbols onto it with a pin, e.g. a heart for a love spell.

- Gaze into the candle to meditate on your intention.

- Anoint the candle with oils that suit your aims.

- Place crystals and herbs, chosen for their magical properties, around the candle.

- "Read" the candle flame for divination. Notice if it burns brightly, flickers, smokes or sparks – what do you think these effects mean? Are they giving you a message?

- Use candles of different sizes. Small birthday cake candles are great for a quick spell. Large pillar candles can be lit every day for ongoing spells, daily rituals or meditation.

- Scented candles can add to the atmosphere, and the aromas can affect your mood and, therefore, the spell's effectiveness.

A COMFORTING INFUSION

This spell's ingredients are chosen for their healing and soothing properties, ideal when you're fighting off a cold or flu.

You will need

- 480 ml (16 fl oz) apple juice
- 240 ml (8 fl oz) water
- Orange or lemon – for its immunity-boosting, uplifting qualities
- Star anise – a spice that helps ease symptoms of coughs and colds
- Small piece of fresh ginger to stimulate the senses
- Small piece of lemongrass to boost the immune system
- Pinch each of ground cinnamon (or a cinnamon stick) and nutmeg to evoke comfort
- 1–2 tsp honey (manuka is excellent if you have it) for its antibacterial properties and sweetness
- Camomile teabag to calm and heal
- Cooking pan
- Wooden spoon
- Tea strainer
- Your favourite mug

Method

1. Pour the apple juice and water into the pan and place over a low heat.

2. Squeeze the juice from the orange or lemon and add to the pan.

3. Add the star anise, ginger, lemongrass, cinnamon, honey and camomile teabag.

4. Stir deosil (clockwise) to draw in healing energy.

5. When the potion is warmed, strain it through the tea strainer into your favourite mug and sip slowly, enjoying the comfort and warmth.

Anyone who has loved has been touched by magic. It is such a simple and such an extraordinary part of the lives we live.

NORA ROBERTS

YOU ARE A
FORCE OF
NATURE

WORDS OF POWER

An incantation is a series of words used as a spell or charm. Incantations are great for quick, on-the-spot spells, as you need nothing other than your own energy. Much like an affirmation or mantra, the words reflect your intention. Think of phrases that make you feel strong and capable, and memorize them for when you need them most. Below are some phrases that you might like to try, or better still, use your intuition to create unique incantations.

- "I am whole, I am free, I am safe, I am me."
- "I walk through this moment with wisdom and passion."
- "I am calm and fearless."
- "Strength, wisdom and compassion are mine."
- "I will find kindness here."

Keep a note of your incantations in your grimoire as a reminder.

Casting the spell

To use your incantation, close your eyes and visualize a white light glowing in the centre of your chest. Speak the words as though they are coming directly from this white light. If you are in a situation where it's not possible to speak out loud, repeat the incantation in your mind.

GADGET MAGIC FOR FRIENDSHIP

Although modern witches feel a connection to nature, they are not averse to incorporating modern technology where appropriate. Use this spell to build good communication with a friend.

You will need

- Incense
- Mobile phone
- 2 cardamom seeds

Casting the spell

1. Cleanse your mobile phone by passing it through the smoke of an incense stick.

2. Place your phone on a flat surface.

3. Bring up a picture of your friend on your phone screen and place the cardamom seeds on top (cardamom clears negativity, restoring love and friendship).

4. Set a timer for 2 minutes, then bring the photo back to the screen. (The number two in numerology represents partnerships and brings peace and balance to relationships.)

5. When the timer goes off, remove the cardamom seeds and send a heartfelt message to that friend asking how they are, paying them a compliment or telling them how much you appreciate them.

A SPELL FOR LETTING GO AND MOVING ON

This spell will help you to banish unwanted emotions and elements from your life that are no longer serving you well.

You will need

- White candle for cleansing in a safe candleholder
- Lavender oil for happiness
- Cauldron or fireproof dish on a heatproof mat
- Dried marjoram for moving on
- Dried thyme for healing
- Garlic salt for inner strength and banishing negativity
- Piece of white paper and a black pen

Casting the spell

1. Anoint your candle with a drop of lavender oil and light it.

2. Place a generous pinch of herbs and garlic salt into your cauldron or dish.

3. Stir the herbs in a widdershins (counter-clockwise) direction while thinking of things you wish to release and let go of.

4. Write these things onto the paper.

5. Sprinkle the herb mix onto the paper and fold it up, keeping the herbs inside.

6. Safely light the paper from the candle and place it into the cauldron or heatproof dish. As you watch it go up in flames, feel the relief of letting go and notice how you are now ready to move on.

7. Once the ashes are cold, throw them in the bin; this symbolizes the things you have released being disposed of.

Cast this spell during the waning moon to draw on its powers of reducing and removing.

CAREER CANDLE

Use this spell when you need a helping hand with your career.

You will need

- Cauldron or bowl
- 30 ml (2 tbsp) almond oil for prosperity and wisdom
- Pinch or drop of the following dried herbs, spices and oils according to your needs:
- Thyme for business success
- Nutmeg for luck
- Cinnamon for power
- Fennel seeds for courage and inner strength
- Tarragon for self-confidence
- Citronella for clear thinking
- Chilli powder for new ideas
- Dill for overcoming obstacles
- Ginger for money and success
- Small bottle or jar
- Orange candle (a birthday candle size will do)

Casting the spell

1. In your cauldron or a suitable bowl, mix together the almond oil and your chosen ingredients.

2. Stir in a deosil (clockwise) direction to draw in the qualities you seek to evoke.

3. Pour this potion into a small bottle or jar and keep it for when needed.

4. On a day when you need extra help with your career (e.g. before an interview), anoint an orange candle with the potion and light it in a safe place.

5. Gaze into the flame while visualizing your success.

A SPELL TO KEEP THE PEACE

Family get-togethers can be a source of tension, so create a positive vibe by choosing your ingredients for this spell according to what you feel will benefit your family.

You will need

- Small jar, bottle or drawstring bag
- Tiny rose quartz crystal or pink pebble to represent unconditional love

Choose a few of the following ingredients:

- Dried lavender for healing
- Lemon balm to reduce stress
- Valerian for peaceful relationships
- Catnip for fun
- Chives for a positive outlook
- Camomile for calmness
- Nutmeg for luck
- Rosemary for positivity

Casting the spell

1. Place the crystal and herbs into the jar, bottle or bag, thinking of their properties and intending these qualities will be abundant at your family gathering.

2. Place the lid on the jar or tighten the bag strings while thinking or saying: "Gratitude to the spell within for bringing your peace to my kin. It is the will of my heart, and so it shall be."

3. Place this spell jar or bag in the room where you will be spending time together or carry it with you.

SPELL FOR REKINDLING LOVE

Use this spell when you feel your relationship needs some loving attention.

You will need

- 2 pink birthday candles
- Pin
- Drop of honey to bring sweetness and healing
- Patchouli oil for passion and/or jasmine oil for romance
- Cinnamon powder for love
- Dried valerian and/or lemon balm for healing and love
- Tea light in a heatproof holder
- 2 rose quartz crystal chips

Casting the spell

1. Etch your name into one of the pink candles and your partner's name into the other using the pin.

2. Mix the honey and oils together and smear some onto the sides of each pink candle.

3. Sprinkle the herbs and spices onto the pink candles.

4. Light the tea light and gaze into the flame, visualizing happy times ahead.

5   Hold the pink candles side by side, so they touch, and light them from the tea light.

6. Keeping the pink candles touching, press them into the soft wax of the tea light (which will extinguish the tea light).

7. Drop the crystals into the tea light wax beside the pink candles.

8. Watch the flames burn together while you contemplate your gratitude for the relationship.

TO BREAK A HABIT

Chives are believed to be great for habit-breaking. Draw on their powers to help you break an unhelpful habit.

You will need

- Recycled tissue paper (a sheet of kitchen paper will do)
- Black pen
- 5 chives

Casting the spell

1. During a waning moon, write your habit onto the centre of the paper.

2. Place the chives around the writing in the shape of a pentagram.

3. Scrunch up the paper and chive stalks while thinking about how this habit does not serve you well and why you want to be rid of it.

4. Bury the paper in the soil.

5. Hold the intention that as the spell decays, your habit will fade.

*Being a witch means
living in this world
consciously, powerfully,
and unapologetically.*

GABRIELA HERSTIK

YOU ARE
MAGICAL;
YOU ARE
POWERFUL

TRAVEL TALISMAN

The ingredients for this spell are chosen for qualities such as protection, confidence, luck, inner strength and adventurous spirit.

Include a few of the following dried herbs and spices:

- Cumin seeds
- Feverfew
- Allspice
- Tarragon
- Black peppercorns

- Sage
- Fennel
- Cloves
- Rosemary

Pick a crystal that appeals to you. The best ones for travel are:

- Aquamarine
- Malachite
- Labradorite

- Black tourmaline
- Yellow jasper

Casting the spell

1. Place your ingredients and crystal, along with some dust or dirt from your home, into a small drawstring bag or pouch.

2. Say the words "Carry me safely, with adventure and fun, and return me home when I am done" into the bag. Tie the top tightly to seal.

3. Tie on a pentacle charm for added protection.

4. Carry the talisman on you when you travel. You could wear it on a cord hanging around your neck, keep it in your pocket or tuck it into your luggage.

PROSPERITY OIL

Burn frankincense while making this prosperity oil to open the abundant gifts you deserve.

You will need

- 30 ml (1 fl oz) almond carrier oil
- 4 drops each patchouli and orange essential oils

Casting the spell

1. Add the drops of patchouli and orange oils to the almond oil, stirring deosil (clockwise).

2. Dip your finger into the oil and press it onto the centre of your forehead.

3. Say a prosperity affirmation to yourself. Pick one of the following or create your own.
   - "I welcome an abundant flow of money."
   - "I deserve the peace of mind that an abundant flow of money brings."
   - "I enjoy the security of an abundant income."
   - "Money comes easily to me."

4. Keep the oil in a small bottle so that you can use it whenever you feel you need to.

> To attract money, put a drop of prosperity oil onto a small citrine crystal and keep it in your wallet.

FRIENDSHIP CAKE

Bake this delicious fruit loaf for gatherings with friends. The spices are chosen for their ability to nurture friendships, making it perfect for circle gatherings.

You will need

- 65 g (2 oz) whole grain cereal
- 100 g (4 oz) mixed, dried fruit
- 150 g (5 oz) sugar
- 240 ml (8 fl oz) milk (any kind)
- 125 g (4 oz) self-raising flour
- 1 tsp poppy seeds
- ½ tsp ground nutmeg
- ½ tsp ground cinnamon
- ½ tsp ground cardamom
- Candle
- Lined loaf tin

Method

1. Light a candle while you bake, symbolizing the love and light you are pouring into the cake. Place the cereal, sugar and dried fruit into a mixing bowl, pour over the milk, stir and let sit for a few minutes.

2. Add the flour, poppy seeds and spices. Stir until combined.

3. Transfer the mixture to a lined loaf tin. Bake at 180°C/356°F for 1 hour.

4. Check the cake is cooked and adjust the time to suit your oven.

5. Slice and serve as it is or spread with butter.

Each time you mix the cake, stir deosil (clockwise) to attract positivity, and visualize your loving energy flowing from your hand, down the spoon and into the cake.

BANISHING SPELL

Freeze someone out of your life with this quick and easy spell. We all try to exercise tolerance and compassion, but this spell is for situations where you feel safer to cut ties with a person, wishing them no harm, but to go your separate ways.

You will need

- Sage leaf or piece of paper
- Black pen
- Small dish
- Water

Casting the spell

1. Write the name of the person you wish to remove from your life onto the leaf or paper.

2. Place it into the dish and pour over enough water to cover the leaf.

3. Place the dish into the freezer and leave for a few hours.

4. Remove the ice from the freezer and take it somewhere where you can throw it as far as possible. Alternatively, if you can't get out or worry about the ice melting too quickly, flush it down the toilet. As you dispose of the frozen leaf, visualize this person drifting out of your life.

SWEET LIFE POPPET

A poppet is traditionally a doll used to represent yourself or someone else in a spell. Attract to yourself all the sweetness life has to offer with this poppet spell.

You will need

- Home-baked or shop-bought gingerbread person (to bake your own, follow an online recipe or cookbook)

- Selection of sweet treats, for example, honey, chopped fresh fruit, dried fruits, small sweets, syrup, chocolate sauce, sprinkles, etc.

- Yellow candle

- Your favourite plate

Casting the spell

1. Cut out and bake the gingerbread person according to your recipe's instructions. If you don't have a home-baked or shop-bought gingerbread person, use a cookie cutter to cut out a person shape from a slice of bread. This is your poppet: it represents you in this spell, so be kind and gentle.

2. Light the yellow candle to represent joy and happiness.

3. Carefully place your poppet onto the plate near the candle, so it is bathed in candlelight.

4. Gently pour the honey, syrup or sauce over your poppet and sprinkle on the sweet goodies.

5. Say, "I am open to gratefully receiving life's sweetness."

6. Mindfully enjoy eating your sweet poppet, knowing you deserve all the good things life offers.

SELF-LOVE WITH ROSE

Draw on the nurturing energy of rose quartz and rose oil to support your self-love journey.

You will need

- Pink candle
- Rose essential oil (or rose water)
- Rose quartz tumble stone

Casting the spell

1. Light the pink candle to represent self-love.

2. Put a drop of rose oil (or rose water) onto the forefinger of your dominant hand and press it to the centre of your forehead and say, "I think about myself with love, kindness and respect."

3. Press another drop of rose oil to your throat and say, "I talk about myself with love, kindness and respect."

4. Press a third drop of oil to your heart and say, "I deserve love, kindness and respect, and I find it within and without."

5. Place a drop of the oil onto the rose quartz and carry it close to you in a pocket to remind you to be loving, kind and respectful to yourself.

HOUSE BLESSING

Use this spell to freshen the energy in your home and bring in blessings.

You will need

- Stone to represent north (earth)
- Incense to represent east (air)
- Candle to represent south (fire)
- Seashell to represent west (water) – or find other suitable correspondences for the four quarters

Casting the spell

1. Light the incense and candle and arrange them inside your front door on a fireproof tray or plate with the stone and shell.

2. Open your door and say, "Spirits of earth, water, air and fire, you are welcome here to inspire. Guardians of the north, south, east and west protect this home and keep it blessed."

3. Close the door and say, "Your blessings will stay with me, with love and thanks, so mote it be."

4. Walk around your home with the incense and candle, allowing the light and smoke into every corner.

> **"So mote it be"** means **"so may it be"** and is a common expression in witchcraft to round off a spell.

WISE, MERRY AND BLESSED BE

*The magic we produce comes
from within and around us, not
from looking the correct way or
having the fanciest tarot cards.*

HARMONY NICE

COURAGE SPELL

This spell uses an iron nail because iron is a symbol of bravery and determination. If you can't get hold of one, a steel nail will work as it'll give you "nerves of steel".

You will need

- Red candle
- 30 ml (2 tbsp) olive oil
- 4 drops fennel essential oil
- 4 drops basil essential oil
- Iron nail

Casting the spell

1. Light the red candle to invoke courage.

2. Mix the essential oils into the olive oil.

3. Dip the nail into the oil and use it to gently draw a pentagram on the centre of your chest – make sure you use the side of the nail rather than the tip and be careful not to hurt yourself.

4. Rub the oil into your skin and feel yourself absorbing its courageous properties.

Do not use this oil blend during pregnancy.

LOVE LETTER SPELL

Attract a romantic partner into your life with this love letter.

You will need

- Piece of pink or red paper and a pen (or white paper and a pink or red pen)
- 1 tsp honey for goodness and attraction
- Pinch of ground cinnamon for love
- Rose oil for love and romance
- Pink or red candle for love, passion and romance
- Cauldron or fireproof dish

Casting the spell

1. Write a letter to the universe or any higher power to send you a romantic partner. In the letter, thank the higher power for sending you the person of your dreams and list the qualities that you will love about them.

2. Read the letter aloud, drizzle it with honey and sprinkle over the cinnamon and a few drops of rose oil.

3. Take your letter, candle and cauldron outside or open the windows wide to let the smoke out. Fold the letter up and light it from the candle. Drop it into the cauldron and, as it burns, watch the smoke carry your message away.

LEMON ZING SPELL

Bring the zingy, bright energy and positive vibes of lemon to a room such as your bedroom, living room or office and remove negativity with this simple spell.

You will need

- Lemon
- Knife
- Four small bowls

Casting the spell

1. Cut a lemon into quarters and place a piece in each bowl.

2. Place a bowl of lemon in each corner of your room. Enjoy the fresh scent as the lemon gives out its positive vibes.

3. Keep an eye on your lemon pieces – after a while, they will absorb the negative energy and start to go black. Remove them when they begin to mould and throw them away.

> **Did you know?** Placing a line of salt across a door stops negativity from entering.

CONFIDENCE RITUAL BATH

Relax in a bath scented with oils chosen to boost your confidence.

You will need

- Camomile tea
- Slice of lemon
- Strip of orange zest
- Lavender, bergamot, jasmine and orange essential oils

- Orange candle or tea lights in orange holders
- An hour of uninterrupted time in the bath and plenty of hot water

Casting the spell

1. Make yourself a camomile tea and add the lemon slice and orange zest.

2. Run your bath, adding 3 drops of each essential oil. If you have sensitive skin, you might prefer to drop the oils into the candles or an oil burner instead.

3. Safely light your candle(s).

4. Slip into the bath and sip your tea while you enjoy the warm water and its confidence-boosting aromas.

> **Boost this spell by saying positive affirmations to yourself in the bath. You could try "I am boldly me" or "I am confident and happy."**

RIVER OF MONEY MEDITATION SPELL

Visit a river or the ocean and notice how currents and tides bring new things to the shore and carry old things away. Contemplate the constancy of the flow or tidal rhythm. Recognize that money is just like the river or ocean; it ebbs and flows but is always there, passing through your life. Understand money is just an energy, neither bad nor good; it's what we do with it that has positive or negative effects.

Let go of:

- Negative ideas about money being in relationship to your self-worth.
- The idea you have to work to exhaustion to deserve money.
- The guilt associated with wanting/needing money.

- The need to hold onto money for fear of not replacing it.
- Habits around spending money to mask unhappiness.

Trust that you can make good, safe decisions about money in accordance with your values and priorities. Feel gratitude for the money that flows through your life, recognizing that when it flows out, you gain something in exchange.

HEALING POWDER

The herbs, crystals and oils in this spell are chosen for their general healing properties, but you can look up specific ailments and use the ingredients you feel drawn to in order to personalize your spell.

You will need

- Green candle
- Bowl and spoon
- 1 tbsp salt
- Generous pinch of dried camomile
- Generous pinch of dried lemon balm
- Generous pinch of dried thyme
- Lavender essential oil
- Amethyst tumble stone
- Clear quartz tumble stone
- Jasper tumble stone
- Small jar with a lid and/or a drawstring cloth bag

Casting the spell

1. Light the green candle to signify the healing energy you are drawing in.

2. Mix the ingredients together in the bowl, stirring deosil (clockwise) and ask the universe/any higher powers to pour healing energy into your spell, remembering to thank them.

3. Keep the mixture in a jar or bag with your chosen crystals.

4. To use your healing powder, you can carry it in a pocket or place it into your bath and soak in its healing magic.

A WITCH BOTTLE FOR A HAPPY HOME

This makes a lovely housewarming gift. You will need a small bottle or jar with a wide enough neck to fit everything through. Choose what to put into your bottle according to what you wish to attract to the home. Some ideas are listed below.

- Birthday candle – light, happiness

- Cardamom seed – love, friendship

- Dried lavender head – health, calmness

- Bay leaf – good fortune, strength, wisdom

- Black peppercorn – purification, inner strength

- Dried marigold – comfort, remembering ancestors

- Rice – nourishment, luck

- Tiny bell – music, good communication

- Glitter – sparkle, magic

- Salt – protection and flavour

- Sugar – sweetness

- Small piece of string tied in a loop – family circle, loose ends tied up

- Small clear quartz or other crystal(s)

Place everything into your bottle and speak your wishes for the home into it. Place the lid on tightly and keep it in the room that feels like the heart of your home.

FOLLOW YOUR
INTUITION;
IT'S YOUR
SUPERPOWER

Witchcraft is fun. It offers us a chance to play, to act silly, to let the inner child come out.

STARHAWK

HAPPINESS SPELL

Lift your spirits and make your energy fizz with this spell drawing on the energy of the sun and sunflowers.

You will need

- Yellow candle
- 7 sunflower seeds
- Your favourite feel-good song

Casting the spell

1. Light the yellow candle to represent the energy of the sun and the emotions of joy and happiness.

2. Gaze into the flame and meditate on how it can hold many emotions within you simultaneously and opposing emotions do not have to cancel each other out.

3. Hold the sunflower seeds and say these affirmations, eating a sunflower seed after each one.

   - "I deserve happiness."
   - "Right now, I choose joy."
   - "I give myself permission to be happy."
   - "I am allowed to enjoy myself."
   - "I am capable of great happiness."
   - "I am grateful for my many reasons to be happy."
   - "Happiness shines from within me."

4. Play your feel-good song and dance, sing and let your happiness show.

5. Plan something to look forward to that makes you happy – a walk in nature, your favourite film or a gathering with friends.

SLEEPY SPELL

Help yourself drift off into a deep, refreshing sleep by drawing on the relaxing powers of lavender and camomile.

You will need

- 2 tbsp water
- 6 drops lavender essential oil
- Oil burner
- Tea light

- Camomile tea
- Dried lavender
- Dried camomile
- Circle of fabric
- Ribbon

Casting the spell

1. Place the water and lavender oil on the oil burner and light the tea light underneath.

2. Make yourself a cup of camomile tea. Sip your tea and enjoy the lavender scent as you create your sleep pouch.

3. To create your sleep pouch, place the dried herbs in the centre of the fabric circle and draw up the sides. Tie the ribbon around the fabric to keep the herbs inside and secure with a tight knot.

4. Place the pouch under your pillow.

5. When you go to bed, close your eyes and take three deep, relaxing breaths, inhaling the soothing scents of lavender and camomile.

A SPELL TO BOOST WILLPOWER

Use this spell when you need to bolster your resolve.

You will need

- Small drawstring bag
- Amethyst crystal – purifying and protective
- Black onyx crystal – supportive, calming and confidence boosting
- Carnelian crystal – gives you the strength to resist, courage and self-worth
- 1 tsp black peppercorns – inner strength and protection
- 1 tsp dried tarragon – self-confidence
- 1 tsp dried rosemary – banishes negativity
- 1 tsp dried chives – for breaking bad habits
- Bay leaf – for success and wisdom

Casting the spell

1. Place the crystals and herbs into the bag, keeping personal resolve in mind, and tie the top tightly.

2. Carry it in your pocket or bag on occasions when your willpower needs a bit of support.

If you're heading out to a social event where others will be drinking alcohol, and you don't want to, take this spell with you to help you avoid temptation.

DREAM RECALL POUCH

Dreams tell you a lot about what's going on in your subconscious, but it's often hard to remember them in the morning. This spell helps you recall and understand your dreams.

You will need

- Purple fabric roughly 20 cm (6 in.) square (purple symbolizes spiritual wisdom)
- Needle and thread or glue
- Eucalyptus leaves for lucid dreaming
- Bay leaf for wisdom
- Juniper berries for psychic awareness

- Lapis lazuli crystal for psychic awareness and intuition
- Red jasper crystal for dream recall
- Notebook to use as a dream journal
- Pen

Casting the spell

1. Fold the fabric in half and sew or glue two of the open sides together.

2. Place the leaves, berries and crystals in the pouch.

3. Sew or glue the last side together.

4. At bedtime, place the pouch under your pillow and the book and pen beside your bed.

5. First thing in the morning, before you do anything else, write what you remember about your dreams in the journal.

After a while, you may start noticing patterns and themes in your dreams. What do they mean to you? You can look up dream meanings, but your own intuition can tell you a lot.

EVERGREEN WINTER SOLSTICE SPELL

Winter solstice, the shortest day and longest night of the year, is the darkest point in the calendar but represents the sun's rebirth, as from this point on, the days start to lengthen. To brighten your mood, decorate your home with evergreen foliage to remind you that lush, fertile, sunny days will return. Traditional evergreens for winter solstice include holly, ivy, mistletoe and fir but choose whatever is local and meaningful to you. Use this time of stillness to contemplate the year ahead.

You will need

- Evergreen leaves retained from the season's celebrations
- Gold pen
- Cauldron or fireproof dish

Casting the spell for the year ahead

1. Take a moment with the leaves in your hands to give them your gratitude for their bright presence and the positive energy they brought to your home.

2. With a gold pen, write your wishes for the year ahead onto the leaves.

3. Burn your leaves outside in a cauldron, fireproof dish, campfire or fire pit and allow the firelight to bring you cheer.

SUMMER SOLSTICE CHARM

The summer solstice is the longest day and shortest night, when the sun is considered at the height of its powers. Many witches like to stay up all night to see the sunrise on the solstice. Use the power of the rising solstice sun to charge a charm so that you can carry the energy of the sun with you always.

You will need

- Hag stone pendant (see page 24)

Casting the spell

1. As the sun rises on the summer solstice, hold the stone up so that the sun's light shines through the hole onto you.

2. Say, "Solstice sun, I call you to light my sacred fire within. Charge this stone with your light and powers, so it may bless my darkest hours. With love and gratitude, so mote it be." This will bless both you and the stone with the sun's energy and can help give you the boost you need if you suffer from low mood in the winter.

SPRING EQUINOX RITUAL

The two equinoxes fall directly between the summer and winter solstices and are the days of equal light and dark. From the spring equinox, the days get longer than the nights, so it is a time of growth and rebirth. Eggs, flowers and baby animals are used at this time as symbols of fertility, hope and nature's abundance.

Casting the spell

1.   Light a candle or a circle of candles all around you.

2.   Curl into a ball as though you are inside an egg and contemplate how your winter self has been. Have you felt the need to hibernate? Now is the time to come out of your winter shell and blossom.

3.   Slowly stretch out each limb, one at a time, and visualize yourself breaking out of the eggshell (taking care not to knock over any candles).

4.   Gradually come to your feet and stand tall, legs wide, in a strong stance. Stretch your arms over your head and slowly bring them to your sides, feeling how wide they stretch and enjoying taking up space.

5.   Take a step forward to symbolize you stepping into the next phase of your life, taking your wisdom and strength with you.

*Being a witch isn't what
you do, it's who you are.*

LISA LISTER

KEEP SOME
ROOM IN
YOUR HEART
FOR MAGIC

AUTUMN OFFERING SOUP

At the autumn equinox, it's common for witches to leave offerings to their ancestors. Contemplate your line of ancestors and the strength, resilience and love that has led to you being here while you enjoy this hearty soup.

You will need

- 1 kg (2 lb) pumpkin, peeled and cubed
- Onion, chopped
- 60 g (2 oz) butter or oil
- 1 litre (34 fl oz) chicken or vegetable stock
- 1 tsp grated ginger
- 1 tsp chopped parsley
- Pinch of allspice for healing and compassion
- 185 ml (6 fl oz) cream or coconut milk
- Salt and pepper for flavour and protection

Method

1. In a large pan, gently fry the pumpkin and onion in the butter or oil for 15 minutes.

2. Add the stock, ginger, parsley and allspice, cover and simmer for 20 minutes or until the pumpkin is tender.

3. Allow to cool, then blend until smooth.

4. Return to the heat and stir in the cream or coconut milk, and season to taste.

5. Place a small bowlful on your altar or dinner table as an offering to your ancestors.

NEW MOON SPELL

A vision board represents your desires, which aids you in visualizing and manifesting your best life. Create yours at the new moon to draw on its energy of new beginnings and potential.

You will need

- Piece of cardboard (the side of a cereal packet works well)
- Scissors and old magazines to cut out pictures and words that represent the things/feelings you wish to manifest
- Pens
- Glue
- Stickers, glitter, pressed flowers, and anything else you wish to add decoration

Casting the spell

1. At the new moon, write on your card: "Like the moon, I am whole, even when I am in darkness." Follow this with your intention, then the words, "With love and gratitude, it will be so," and sign off with your signature.

2. Arrange your chosen images and words on the card (you will cover the writing, but it is still there, empowering your vision board).

3. Glue everything in place and decorate with stickers, glitter, etc., if you wish.

4. Place your vision board where you will see it and be inspired daily.

FULL MOON SELF-LOVE SPELL

The full moon is considered the most magical phase. Charge water, crystals and other spell ingredients with lunar energy by leaving them outdoors or on a windowsill at full moon. They then carry lunar energy into the spells you use them for.

You will need

- Glass bottle of water (rainwater is best, but mineral or tap water is fine)
- Moonlit spot (outdoors or indoors)
- White tissue/cloth
- Mirror

Casting the spell

1. Leave your bottle of water in the moonlight all night at full moon to create moon water.

2. Put some moon water onto a white tissue or cloth and use it to clean your mirror.

3. Stand sky clad (naked) in front of your mirror and appreciate what you can see.

4. Dip the forefinger of your dominant hand into the water and touch it to each part of your body.

5. Starting at your feet and working your way up, say something complimentary or grateful about each part as you go – for example, "I like my dainty toes," or "Thank you, sturdy legs, for carrying me around."

A witch is only as powerful as the love she gives herself.

JULIET DIAZ

YOU DESERVE
MAGIC AND
MIRACLES

LAST WORD

Whether you are a seasoned witch or are just starting out on your witchy path, always remember that the way is yours to walk as you wish. It could be that you view witchcraft as your religion or spirituality or cast spells as a way of exercising your will and building your self-esteem. You might invite higher powers in or only draw on your inner strength. You could be part of a coven or witch alone. You might be out of the broom cupboard or prefer to witch in secrecy. Those choices are yours and yours alone to make and change according to your heart's will.

The spells in this book give you some idea of how to create magic for yourself, but magic isn't confined to spells – you have your unique magic within you. It's your vim and verve, mojo, personal power, will, spirit, pep, fizz, chi, sparkle, pizazz, zip, your true colours, your authenticity, the very essence of you. Only you can shine that special light, that magic that you were born with.

Witchcraft gives you so many opportunities to sprinkle your very own magic around you as you walk through life. Learn about the elements of spell work that interest you, be it herbs, crystals, folklore, etc. And look for ways to use your knowledge and intuition to personalize every spell, ritual, and even mundane tasks, as your personal magic will truly empower your witchcraft. And in turn, your witchcraft will empower you, building your confidence and self-love, supporting you through relationships and careers and all of life's adventures.

Witch wisely, witch kindly, witch your own way.

Merry, bright and blessed be.

SPELL INDEX

Spells for...

IMAGE CREDITS

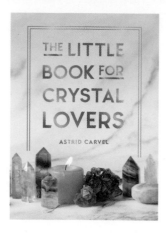

The Little Book
for Crystal Lovers

Astrid Carvel

Paperback

ISBN: 978-1-80007-643-3

Harness the incredible
power of crystals

Enhance your everyday life by discovering the practical and spiritual benefits of crystals. Featuring detailed profiles on dozens of stones, these pages contain everything you need to know to feel the full force of these natural treasures.

The Baby Witch's Journal

Astrid Carvel

Paperback

ISBN: 978-1-80007-714-0

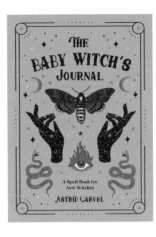

Delve into the magickal world of spells and white witchcraft with this informative and friendly guide for baby witches

Calling all baby witches! Have you ever wanted to develop your intuitive powers to look into the future and manifest your dreams? Are you interested in learning how to harness the moon's power to cast the most potent spells for love and happiness? Or maybe you're just curious about all this witchy stuff and want to know more? If so, this journal is for you!

With easy-to-follow spells and rituals for every occasion, and grimoire pages to record the spells you have cast and any that you've devised yourself, this beautifully designed journal will set you on the path to discovering your true witchy self.

Have you enjoyed this book? If so, find us on Facebook at **Summersdale Publishers**, on Twitter at **@Summersdale** and on Instagram and TikTok at **@summersdalebooks** and get in touch. We'd love to hear from you!

www.summersdale.com